Best Soccer Players of All Time

LARRY EDWARDS

Best Soccer Players of All Time

The game of soccer is the world's most celebrated sports on the planet. For many years this world-class sport has seen some exceptional talent by some of the best athletes competing side-by-side in a number of competitions such as the Euro Cup, The South American Championship, and The World Cup which is held every four years.

There is no doubt that all of the talented players who have ever played the game are great in their own respect. But to become one of the greatest players of all time, a player must contribute more to the game than just the number of goals scored.

To be considered one of the greatest, a talented professional soccer player should also be seen as a club legend or national hero who has contributed greatly to the success of his nation.

Based on this standard, here are our 10 Best Soccer Players of All Time.

1.Pelé (Brazil 🇧🇷)

Pele (1)

Pelé is the winner of the 1958, 1962 and the 1970 World Cup. Pelé's real name is Edson Arantes do Nascimento. He has been often called the best soccer player ever to set foot on the soccer field.

Pelé dribbling past a defender during Malmoe-Brazil 1-7 by Bonkers. (2)

For most of his years since the age of 15, Pelé has played for the Brazilian professional soccer club Santos FC. He then joined the New York Cosmos for a short time after coming out of semi-retirement. Pelé during his career had a record 541 league goals. He is listed by the Guinness World Records as the person with the most career goals scored in soccer history. Pelé has scored a total of 1281 goals in 1363 games.

2. Lionel Messi
(Argentina 🇦🇷)

Lionel Messi. (3)

Born on June 24, 1987, the Argentine soccer player Lionel Andrés "Leo" Messi Cuccittini is nicknamed the Atomic Flee. Messi joined the Spanish soccer club Barcelona at the age of just 13 years old.

By the time Messi had reached the age of 21, he had received the nomination for the Ballon d'Or and FIFA World Player of the Year 2008. He won both awards a year later in 2009.

Messi has amazing dribbling skill. (4)

Lionel Messi is the only player ever to top-score in four back-to-back Champions League campaigns. Messi has the record for the most hat-tricks scored in the competition. He is the youngest Argentine to have played and scored in the 2006 World Cup and won an Olympic Gold Medal in 2007. Messi is quickly challenging Pelé for the crown as the greatest ever soccer player.

3. Maradona (Argentina 🇦🇷)

Maradona in 2007 along with Ricardo Bochini. (5)

Maradona's real name is Diego Armando Maradona Franco. The Argentine Soccer player played in four FIFA World Cups including the 1986 World Cup where he captained the Argentine team to a victory over West Germany. Maradona was awarded the Golden Ball as the best player in the tournament for that year.

Maradona, World Cup 1986, Argentina-Italia 1-1. (6)

Maradona was one of soccer's most controversial players. He was suspended in 1991 for 15 months after failing a drug test in Italy. He was sent home from the 1994 World Cup after testing positive for substance abuse of the stimulant ephedrine.

4. Cristiano Ronaldo (Portugal )

Cristiano Ronaldo. (7)

Cristiano Ronaldo was born on February 5, 1985. His real name is Cristiano Ronaldo dos Santos Aveiro. Cristiano Ronaldo is a Portuguese forward player for the Spanish Club La Liga Real Madrid.

In 2007 Cristiano Ronaldo became the first player in England to win all four of the FWA and PFA awards. He was also the first Portuguese player to win the FIFA/Baloon d'Or award in 2008 and 2013.

Pato Sosa vs Ronaldo. (8)

In 2009 Cristiano Ronaldo became the most expensive soccer player when he changed club from Manchester United to Real Madrid. There he became the first European player to reach a total of 40 goals in a single season and the fastest Real Madrid player to score 100 league goals.

5.Ronaldo (Brazil 🇧🇷)

Ronaldo in 2005. (9)

Ronaldo was born on September 18, 1976. The real name of this Brazilian soccer player is Ronaldo Luis Nazário de Lima. Ronaldo is known by most experts as one of the greatest soccer players of all time.

Ronaldo scoring the winning penalty for Barcelona in the 1997 UEFA Cup Winners Cup Final against Paris Saint-Germain. (10)

Ronaldo is one of the only three men to have ever won the FIFA World Player of the Year award more than three times along with Lionel Messi and Zinedine Zidane.

6.Franz Beckenbauer (Germany ▬)

Franz "Der Kaiser" Beckenbauer. (11)

Franz Anton Beckenbauer is a former German player, coach and manager who was born on September 11, 1945. He was nicknamed Der Kaiser which means "The Emperor" because of his elegant style.

Muller, Beckenbauer and the coach Schon in 1974. (12)

Because of his leadership, and dominance on the soccer field, Beckenbauer was twice awarded the European Soccer player of the Year. He is respected as one of the best German soccer players and one of the 10 best soccer players of all time.

7. Michel Platini (France 🇫🇷)

Michel Platini in Wroclaw in 2009" (13)

Michel Platini was born on June 21, 1955. He is known as the European champion for club and county after winning the European Championship with France in 1984 and the European Cup a year later in 1985.

Michel Platini, president of UEFA, is at Gibraltar Rock Cup 2014.
(14)

Michel François Platini plays as an attacking midfielder. He is one of the best passers, and also is a specialist in free-kicks and goal scoring in the history of soccer. He holds the record for the most goals scored in European Championship final tournaments in 1984.

8. Zinedine Zidane (France ❙❙❙)

Zinedine Zidane 2008. (15)

Zidane is the former French soccer player and now current coach of the Spanish soccer team Real Madrid Castilla. Zinedine Zidane, nicknamed "Zizou", was born on June 23, 1972. Zidane played as an attacking midfielder for the French national soccer teams Real Madrid and Juventus.

Zinedine Zidane WC 2006. (16)

He was well known for his technique refinement and vision when playing. Zidane was named the best European soccer player of the past 50 years in The UEFA Golden Jubilee online poll Poll in 2004.

9. David Beckham (England +)

Beckham as England captain. (17)

Born on May 2, 1975, David Robert Joseph Beckham is well known for his long range passing and superb bending free-kicks. As a retired soccer English player, David Beckham has played for Real Madrid, Los Angeles Galaxy, Preston North End, Milan, Paris Saint-Germain, Manchester United as well as England's national team. Beckham has the record for the most appearances for an outfield player.

Beckham started his professional soccer career at the age of 17 with Manchester United in 1992. He has won the Premier

League title six times, the FA Cup two times as well as winning the UEFA Champions League in 1999.

Beckham with LA Galaxy in 2012. (18)

Beckham is the first English player to have won league titles in England, Spain, France and the United States. After a 20 year career, Beckham announced his retirement from professional soccer at the end of the 2012-2013 season after playing his final game on May 18, 2013.

10. Roberto Baggio (Italy ▮▮)

Roberto Baggio. (19)

Born on February 18, 1967, Roberto Baggio is a retired Italian soccer player who played for the most part as a second forward or as an attacking midfielder.

Baggio was known as a specialist in playmaking. He was also an expert for his bending free kicks. Roberto Baggio is respected as one of the 10 best soccer players of all time. Baggio was awarded fourth place in the internet poll FIFA Player of the Century. He was also chosen to be in the all-time FIFA World Cup all-star team in 2002.

Roberto Baggio. (20)

Baggio during his career played for Italy in 56 matches and scored a total of 27 goals. He is recognized as the Italy's fourth highest goal scorer.

Image Credit

1. *Pele. Image: Wikimedia.*
2. *Pelé dribbling past a defender during Malmoe-Brazil 1-7 by Bonkers. Image: Wikipedia*
3. *Lionel Messi. Image: Calcio Mercato*
4. *Messi has amazing dribbling skill. Image: LG*
5. *Maradona in 2007 along with Ricardo Bochini. Image: Presidecia*
6. *Maradona, World Cup 1986, Argentina-Italia 1-1. Image: Nazionale Calcio*
7. *Cristiano Ronaldo. Image: wikipedia*
8. *Pato Sosa vs Ronaldo. Image: Jan SOLO*
9. *Ronaldo in 2005. Image: Abu_badali*
10. *Ronaldo scoring the winning penalty for Barcelona in the 1997 UEFA Cup Winners Cup Final against Paris Saint-Germain. Image: Clio64*
11. *Franz "Der Kaiser" Beckenbauer. Image: Madebyr.de*
12. *Muller, Beckenbauer and the coach Schon in 1974. Image: Dutch National Archive,*
13. *Michel Platini in Wroclaw in 2009" by Klearchos Kapoutsis*
14. *Michel Platini, president of UEFA, is at Gibraltar Rock Cup 2014. Image: InfoGibraltar*
15. *Zinedine Zidane 2008 by Raphaël Labbé,*
16. *Zinedine Zidane WC 2006. Image: David Ruddell*
17. *Beckham as England captain. Image: ger1axg*
18. *Beckham with LA Galaxy in 2012 Image: Kunal Shah*
19. *Roberto Baggio. Image: soccer-europe*
20. *Roberto Baggio. Image: fantasista10*

From the Author

Thank you very much for downloading and reading this book. I hope that you find the information useful and interesting.

If you enjoyed the book, please take a moment to share your opinion with other on the book page at
http://www.amazon.com/dp/B00NJ6LH3G

Still craving for more interesting soccer books? I recommend you to check out my other soccer books below that are also available for a great price.

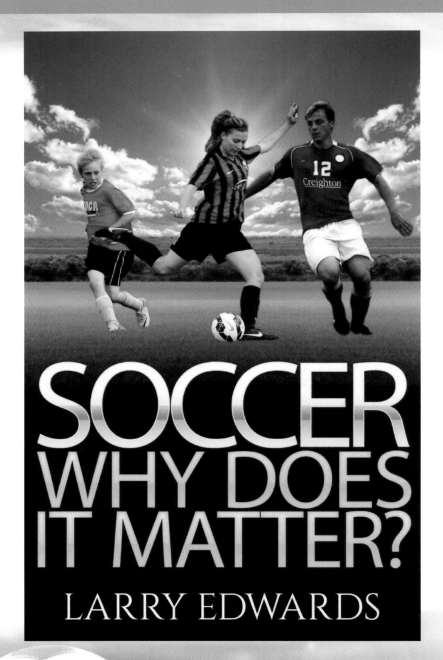

SOCCER
WHY DOES IT MATTER?
LARRY EDWARDS

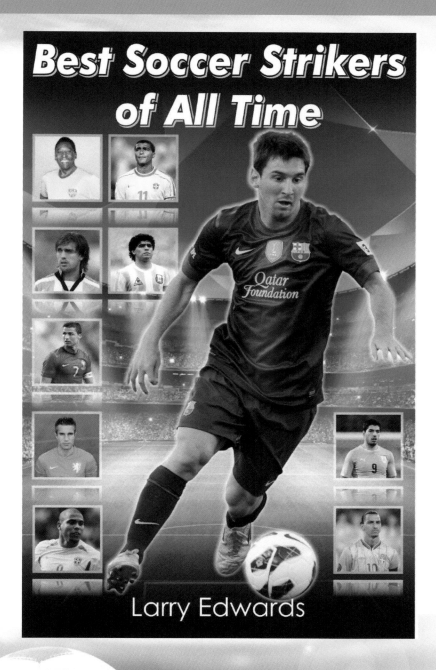

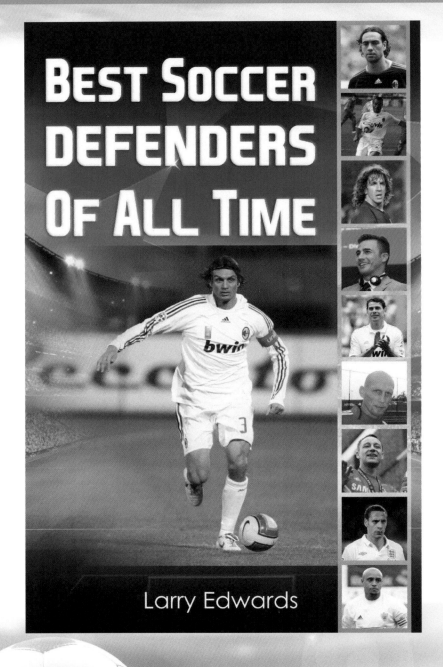

BEST SOCCER DEFENDERS OF ALL TIME

Larry Edwards

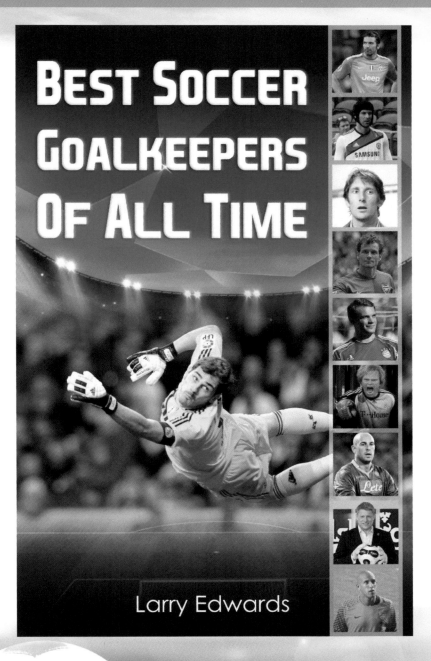

BEST SOCCER GOALKEEPERS OF ALL TIME

Larry Edwards

MESSI

Best Of The Best

Larry Edwards

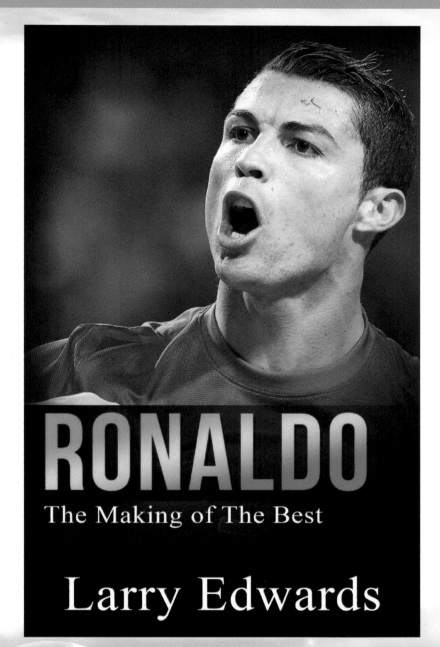

RONALDO
The Making of The Best

Larry Edwards

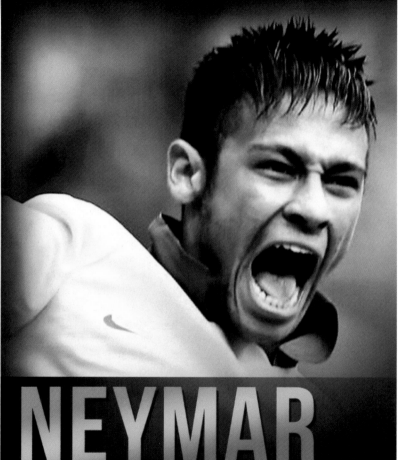

NEYMAR
The Path to Becoming the Best

Larry Edwards

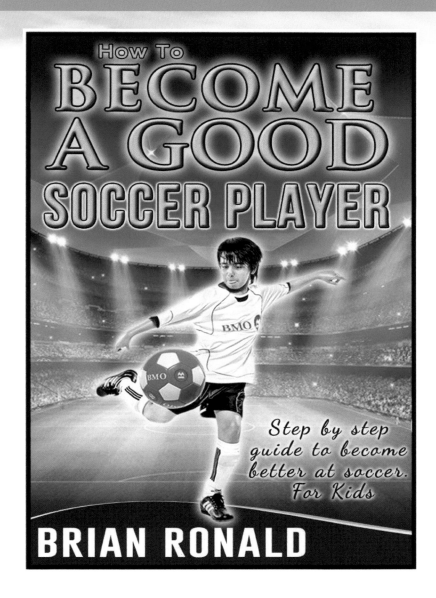

Copyright

CPSIA information can be obtained at www.ICGtesting.com
Printed in the USA
BVIW12n1421230416
445255BV00026B/12

* 9 7 8 1 5 0 8 8 3 1 0 1 3 *